# AFRO AMERICAN ME

# AFRO AMERICAN ME

*by*

Sherryl L. McCorkle

Copyright © 2020, Sherryl L. McCorkle

All rights reserved. Printed in the U.S.A.

No part of this publication may be reproduced
or transmitted in any form or by any means, electronic
or mechanical, including photocopy, recording or any information
storage and retrieval system now known or to be invented,
without permission in writing from the publisher, except
by a reviewer who wishes to quote brief passages in connection
with a review written for inclusion in a magazine,
newspaper or broadcast.

**Quantity Purchases:**
Companies, professional groups, clubs, and other organizations
may qualify for special terms when ordering quantities of this title.
For information, email info@ebooks2go.net,
or call (847) 598-1150 ext. 4141.
www.ebooks2go.net

Published in the United States
by eBooks2go, Inc.
1827 Walden Office Square, Suite 260, Schaumburg, IL 60173

ISBN: 978-1-5457-5113-8

Library of Congress Cataloging in Publication

# Table of Contents

Introduction .................................................................ix

My Father
*Master Tech Sergeant Adolphus Lovell McCorkle Sr.*.................1

My Unforgivable Childhood Memory..........................4

Here I Am ...................................................................8

Swagger......................................................................10

Striptease...................................................................12

I Embrace..................................................................13

Self-Inventory and Awareness Paper...........................14

Test Anxiety ..............................................................16

Gangster Rap's Influence on Inner-City Youth ..........17

Hood .........................................................................19

Peace Won't Be Still ..................................................20

Ghosts .......................................................................21

My Cute Little Handbag............................................22

Beautiful Sleep ..........................................................23

The Sun Will Shine Again ........................................24

Birds .........................................................................25

| | |
|---|---|
| Summer Morning | 26 |
| Writing Therapy | 27 |
| Dayton | 28 |
| From the Master's Hands | 29 |
| Room for Diversity | 30 |
| My Pathway To Success | 31 |
| Single Mothers and the Use of Government Assistance | 33 |

With my deepest gratitude and thanks, I dedicate this book to God, who has made this possible. I would like to thank my family and all those who have supported me in making this accomplishment a reality.

# Introduction

*Afro-American Me* is a literary collection of my poems and essays written while pursuing an associate's degree in mental health/chemical dependency at Sinclair Community College in Dayton, Ohio. I used to think writing papers about self-inventory and awareness was a way of inducing a severe headache. Boy, was I wrong! I learned so much more about myself than I could ever imagine. Attending college has been more than just a higher education; it's been a journey of discovering my true purpose and creative talents.

All my college instructors brought out the best in me. One instructor told me, "Always write what you know about." That advice grew with me, and it's never failed me. My poetry teacher always challenged me to go deeper with my poems. That advice motivated me to rewrite and revise my poems until they become masterpieces. I will never forget the last thing my poetry teacher said to me: "When you write your book, I'd like to have a copy." Every poem and essay I've written has a personal connection—something I know about, a personal experience, how I feel, or my opinion about something.

# My Father
## *Master Tech Sergeant Adolphus Lovell McCorkle Sr.*

---

Adolphus Lovett McCorkle was born February 12, 1930, in High Point, North Carolina. He hated his name, so he changed his name to Anthony Lovell McCorkle. I can honestly say that he lived his life to the fullest. Serving over twenty years in the military, he served in the US Coast Guard, the US Army, and the US Air Force. After retiring from military service in 1968, he made Dayton, Ohio, his place of residence. My father then became a business owner, a teacher in the public education system of Ohio, and was employed with the Regional Transit Authority. This person is so important to me because he was one of the brave who honored his country, was very smart, and family and friends say I'm the spitting image of him.

When I was a teenager, I remember my father telling me how he hated picking cotton every summer as a little boy. I laughed when he told me how he would run and hide when his grandmother would come to get him and his siblings to pick cotton. Every time he saw her coming, he would run and hide. She would call for him, "Come back here, Lovett!" At age thirteen, my dad ran away to join the army. The army didn't find out how old he was until he had served eight years. Most of his youth was spent in the military. I remember him saying, "I've been all over the world, Sherryl." I know that the air force was his favorite military branch. My mom used to say, "He loved to fly those planes!"

After retiring from the air force with an honorable discharge, my father still worked hard. Growing up in the military, he learned and became a certified welder. He opened up his own business called Echo Tool and Die. Whenever he wasn't running his business, he was a parttime math teacher at Garfield, a technical school. I remember asking him what his students were like. "They're recovering drug addicts, women on welfare, or people just getting out of jail," he would say. My father wasn't very talkative at home. He simply said what he had to say and that was that. After retiring from running his business and teaching, he became a bus driver for the Regional Transit Authority. My friends would often tease me about my father being voted the meanest bus driver by them.

My family, my father's friends, and my friends say I'm the spitting image of my father. I am shorter than he was. His height was five foot six; I am five foot two. We both have the same golden-brown complexion and light brown eyes. He always had a fit body, and I stay in shape just like he did. We both have the same birthday, February 12. A good friend of Dad's named Charles Long, who my dad jokingly would call "long head boy" would say, "Sherryl, honey, your daddy spit you out!" He would always tell my brother and me about how smart my dad was and how my father could read blueprints when others couldn't. That reminded me of how I was with my peers growing up. I could do things at school other girls couldn't.

# Afro-American Me

I would show off skating backward in the neighborhood. I started my own cheerleading squad, and I was almost always the line leader in elementary school.

I never got to see my father in his military attire. The pictures I have and the pictures I have seen of him in his military attire are remarkable. He looks so distinguished and proud to serve his country. Whenever Dad wore a suit, work clothes, or casual clothes, he was always neat and handsome. I think his style and mannerisms came from being in the service for so many years. Dirt, filth, wrinkled clothes, unmade beds, dust, and anything out of order was not tolerated by Mr. McCorkle.

My father passed in 2009. I still think about his honorable service years, his hardworking background, and the stand he took for what he truly believed in—America! He will always be important to me because living and trying to apply his principles in my life make me a strong woman.

# My Unforgivable Childhood Memory

I've heard and read many times we must let go and let God. Forgiveness is one of the most difficult obstacles I've ever had to overcome. The most heartbreaking memory took place when I was very young. It took place one fall morning outside of a courtroom door. My brother and I were seated on a long brown bench next to my father's brother, our uncle John. I was seven years old, and my brother was nine years old, so we were too young to go inside the courtroom.

Our uncle John was a short, stubby, dark-skinned man with a big round head. He wore big bifocals, which made him look funny to my brother and me, and we made fun of him whenever his back was turned. Every now and then my uncle would turn his head from the newspaper he was reading, look over his bifocals at us, and say, "Y'all two okay?"

And like an in-sync choir, we both nodded our heads and said, "Um- huh."

My legs were too short to touch the floor. I began to swing my legs back and forth as I started to think hard. Today was mysterious. I had to figure out why my mother woke us up so early in the morning. All she told us to do was get up and get dressed. She said nothing as we got dressed, nothing when we ate breakfast, and nothing on our mysterious drive to the courthouse. What was wrong with my mom?

As I started to fall asleep, leaning toward my uncle John, I was awakened by the courtroom door. As it opened, it slammed against the adjacent wall, and out walked my mother. She had a look of defeat and big tears were rolling down her face. Mother didn't even stop to say anything to my uncle, my brother, or me. She walked right past us at a fast pace; it was like she was power walking. I instantly took off after her. *Where is she going?* I thought. *Why is she leaving without my brother and me?*

"Momma!" I yelled. Maybe she didn't hear me, so I yelled to her again. "Momma, wait!" She kept walking fast. She was getting too far away from me, so I started to run a little to catch up with her. As I got close to her, I grabbed her hand and said, "Momma, I want to go with you!" My eyes started to water, and my nose was burning.

She snatched her hand away and said, "No, go with your father!" She wouldn't even look at me. She looked as if she was trying not to cry. With her voice slowly cracking and breaking up, she said, "Go with him. He can take care of you. I can't—go!" My heart felt like it was in pieces.

"I don't want to. Please, Mommy!" I begged. I watched in disbelief as my mother continued to walk down the sidewalk until I couldn't see her anymore. Then I understood: It was a custody battle. My brother and I had to go live with my father. I didn't want to live with him. I wanted my mom. My tears would not stop falling. How could she let this happen?

As I walked back to the courthouse, I straightened up my face. I had to be a big girl now.

My father had an evil smirk on his face, and my brother's look was nonchalant. Uncle John waved goodbye, so my father, brother, and I went to my father's house to start our lives together without Mom. I hated it. I cried myself to sleep at night. I couldn't eat. I always wondered where she was and if she was safe. I missed her hugs, her smell, and her tucking me in bed at night. I missed her.

Time went on, and finally we started seeing Mom again. She began picking up my brother and me on the weekends and on her days off from work. Mom had been working two jobs, had moved into a nice house, and had two cars. I remembered hugging her so tight when she had to bring us back home to Dad's house. She would always promise, "I'm going to get you and your brother back one day."

I would cry and ask, "Why we just can't stay now, Mommy?"

She would just hug me tightly and say, "I'll be back to get y'all on my next day off." I hated waiting. The time between her days off seemed so long. My heart would mend when she picked my brother and me up and break all over again when she brought us back. As I grew older, I learned to deal with it.

Before she passed away, I got the chance to ask Mom why she gave us to our father. I was about thirty-four years old. I had just gotten off from work, stopped by her house, and felt it was time to get animosity off my chest. She explained that after she and my father divorced, he was court-ordered to pay child support, but he refused to pay it.

Dad wouldn't help with childcare expenses, and he wouldn't help her buy us clothes or food. She explained how, back then, child support was not enforced. Mother also told me that since she and my dad were from

North Carolina, she had no relatives or help in Dayton. She said, "I did what I thought was best. I gave y'all to yo daddy." At that point in my life, I just felt that all those were excuses. It may have been selfish of me, but I felt she didn't understand the pain I went through growing up without her. She wasn't there for the lonely nights I felt scared, the missed school field trips, the school plays, the day I started my period, and all the times my evil stepmother tortured my brother and me with, "Yo momma don't love you; she left you!"

After reminding her of the torment I went through, she said in a soft crackling voice, "I'm sorry for not being there for y'all." Sorry just wasn't helping me at that time. I was still so mad. As I turned my back to walk out her door she said, "The day I left y'all, I had a dream that night. I saw you and your brother sitting in the middle of a bed, and huge flames and smoke surrounded the bed. A big flaming sword was circling around it. A voice told me that I left my children in a burning hell."

In a condescending voice I said, "Yeah, you sure fucking did." I walked out and to this day I wish I could take it back, but I can't. I had to pray and meditate that the unforgivable childhood memory would be truly forgiven in my heart and in my soul. Matthew 18:21–35, in the New King James Version, explains why I must forgive. If I don't forgive, God won't forgive me. I wouldn't be totally honest if I said reading that scripture made it easy for me to let go and let God. Continued prayer and meditation helped me to overcome my anger. Learning to forgive set me free from that pain. It helped me to love and have more compassion for others. I'm a better mother, grandmother, sister, aunt, Christian woman, survivor, and a true warrior in the life God gave me.

# Here I Am

So here I am.

From 5350 Hoover Avenue, my mom nicknamed me Boo. "Don't call me that!" I'd say.
Ms. Helen would say, "She's as cute as a button!" She said it almost every time she saw me.
I would sparkle inside and would give the biggest smile I could give.
That sparkle and smile would soon be tarnished by a merciless voice.
"Ya mammy had you lookin' like a nappy-headed rag doll."
That coldhearted voice would also say,
"Ya mammy don't love you. She gave you away!" What could a seven-year-old say?
A broken heart and spirit as I turned and walked away.
A condemned child grew up and around evil words and hate. Here I am now. Today's a new day.
I can celebrate where I was, where I am, And where I will be.

I can conquer all obstacles and do all things through God who strengthens me.
I was told, "You ain't gon be nothin'!"

Here I am somebody!
I was told, "You can't!"
Here I am, I've proven that I can!

My journey and purpose for God's Kingdom isn't over yet. As long as the master blows breath in me, here I am:
Afro-American me!

# Swagger

I am a forty-one-year-old African American woman. I have three sons, whose ages are twenty-five, twenty, and eighteen. My family, friends, coworkers, and people I meet say I look half my age. The only word I can use to define my go-getter attitude, my natural Dayton native-southern dialect, and why it shows I am so proud and blessed to be an African American woman is swagger.

I seize any opportunity to get what I want. I remember being so terrified to drive a car. Just like I was tired of being on welfare, I was tired of depending on a ride. I needed rides to doctor's appointments, to get groceries, to see my caseworker, to child support, to teacher's conferences, to after school programs, and to unexpected emergencies. I know this had to be annoying for my family and friends. So, in 1998, when I got my first full-time job, eventually I got my first income tax check. At age twenty-six, I seized the opportunity to get my driver's license, and I purchased my first car. Whenever I got behind the steering wheel of my all-white 1986 Pontiac Bonneville Brougham, I'd seize the opportunity to lean back and smile.

I am a Dayton native, but some people say I talk with a slight southern accent and a lot of slang. I was born in Dayton, Ohio. Both of my parents were born and raised in North Carolina, so I have spent some time around country folk. Whenever someone says hello or hi to me, like most country folk, I'll say, "Hey!" or "Hey dere!" At work one day, a coworker looked at me, smiled, and said, "Catchy phrases."

I looked at her strangely and said, "Huh?"

She went on to explain that she couldn't remember where she was, but she heard someone say, "I know dat's right!" and she instantly thought of me. It made me feel good to hear her say, "No one says that like you. That's your phrase!"

I am so blessed and so proud to be an African American woman. Wherever I go, I walk with my head held high, with the biggest and brightest smile on my face, and I step with the coolest, slightly sexy walk that a proud and blessed black woman could have! All my experiences, whether good or bad, have blessed me with the power of wisdom. I am proud and blessed to be the only African American female to receive a scholarship toward my college education from my job this year. I am blessed and proud to have had three sons. Raising them and being on public assistance gave me the motivation to climb!

For my conclusion, I just want to note when defining one's self, the choice of words or characteristics of that person is totally individual. As for myself, Ms. Sherryl Lynn McCorkle, my ingenuity, my attitude, my persistence, my self-esteem, my style, and my flair is swagger!

# Striptease

She takes the catwalk, a lioness queen of the jungle, approaching her stage with mysterious eyes.
Who gets devoured? Who's her prey? As the music begins, her body sways.
She moves seductively to the rhythm. The lighting is dim, creating an ambience of mystique.
Her silhouette graces the spotlight—goddess of the night, sexy ballerina, lady of mystery, sexy senorita.
The gents rejoice in awe.
Visions of her dance serenade their heads. She's their ultimate fantasy. Her pain runs deep, though the gents won't see. The merciless landlord who screams,
"Pay me my rent or get out. This place here ain't for free!" Her pain runs deep, though the gents won't see the children cry out,
"Mommy! Mommy! We hungry. When can we eat?" She dances with emotion. She dances with passion, relieving her tormented soul.
Unleashing the power of her true compassion, she makes love to the music as she coils her body around the pole. She dances. She dances.
For this she knows.
This jungle is hers. She runs the show!

# I Embrace

The scrapes and scratches that won't go away are life's learned lessons from the past and lessons learned today.
I embrace womanhood; I embrace me.
I embrace the natural beauty and power my creator invested in me.
I embrace the low valleys and mountaintops. I remember rough times in the valleys.
I thought I'd never make it to the top. Through the struggles, pain, hard times, and challenges,
I preserve and press on with God—my life balance.
I embrace love thy neighbor as yourself and lending a helping hand to strangers when they need help. I embrace prosperity and common wealth.
I embrace investing in our children, giving to the poor, and compassion for senior citizens who need help. I embrace peace, love, joy, and laughter.
Equality, justice for all, and life ever after.

# Self-Inventory and Awareness Paper

These six paragraphs identify who I am, what I value, my goals, and why I chose mental health/chemical dependency for a career.

I identify myself as a blessed woman of God who wears many hats. My creator blessed me with strength, wisdom, courage, compassion, motivation, and the will to become educated so that I can continue to provide excellent patient-care service for the individuals I help care for. My many hats are a mother, a father, an auntie, a grandmother, a sister, a best friend, a cousin, a coworker, a student, a choir member, and the hats keep changing. What I love most about all these roles I represent is being a natural teacher. At some point, all these roles gave me an opportunity to teach someone how to do something. For example, as a mother, I always demonstrated and taught my sons how to clean the house thoroughly. One interest that keeps me motivated to become a college graduate is to someday obtain foreclosed properties and have them renovated. I would love to start some group homes for the mentally ill who are coming out of treatment facilities and have nowhere to go.

My trust in God is the most important asset in my life. He has kept me, as there have been times I thought it was over for me! Still I stand! My family and their well-being keeps me waking up in the morning, especially when I just don't want to. It is so important to me to be close to my grandson. Loving him is so different from the love I have for my sons. Having balance in my life is essential. Without it, I wouldn't make it. Keeping my life balanced has been difficult at times. I'm going to succeed, so no matter how tough times get, my strength, wisdom, and courage will pull me through. I see my job as an important asset as well. I am truly thankful to have a job, because some people don't.

I decided to become a helper because someone close to my family suffers from a mental illness. Working in this field for six years has truly educated me. I enjoy working with the patients, yet there are times when I experience burnout. There are a lot of people who become homeless because they are put out by family who don't know their family member is suffering from a mental illness. Jails and juvenile detention centers are full of repeat offenders who are mentally ill. This social issue bothers me, and if there is some way I can contribute help to this cause, my education and work in mental health/chemical dependency was the proper choice.

I believe and I value the fact that when working with my coworkers together, we should ensure cleanliness and safety in our milieu at all times. I value teamwork and keep the work atmosphere positive as much as I can. I value healthy relationships at all times with the patients I work with because working on a behavioral health unit can be very dangerous.

# **Test Anxiety**

I sit slowly in my seat. It's on again. I taste defeat. Butterflies attack my belly.

My hands shake, my palms are sweaty. I hate tests. I can't concentrate.

Pass the barf bag—time to regurgitate. My mind is a cloud filled with fluff.

I know I studied.

Why can't I remember this stuff?

The roll call is taken. Tests are passed out.

I take in a deep breath and let it out through my mouth.

My mind starts to focus, and my body begins to settle down.

I take in another deep breath and let it out through my mouth.

Ah! What a relief. I'm coming around. Anxiety before a test drives me insane. Never again will I let it cloud my brain.

Before every test I must calm down—breathe in deep through my nose and let it out through my mouth ...

# Gangster Rap's Influence on Inner-City Youth

Gangster music is very controversial. The subgenre of hip-hop gangster rap has been noted for it's negative influences on inner-city youth. Authority figures, politicians, parents, and religious leaders have tried to ban this music for years. I do agree that gangster music contains lyrics that make criminal activity, violent behavior, and drug use acceptable and appealing.

One influence gangster rap has on inner-city youth is that it makes the "thug life" seem fabulous, and this encourages criminal activity. Gangster rappers often rap about selling marijuana, heroin, and cocaine as a way to get fast money. They also rap about their experiences as drug dealers and how it helped them to survive hard times. Being a thug was also a way gangster rappers became popular and gained respect in the hood. Gangster rapper Gucci Mane spit this lyric: "I stay on some street shit/in love with this beef shit/my diamonds ocean blue so they might get u sea sick/fuck wit dat glock yo sawed off twelve gauge shatty/plus when I aim man I aim for the upper body." Inner-city youth see these gangster rappers in expensive clothes, flashy cars, and jewelry and think that the thug life just might be okay.

Gangster rap can also influence violent behavior. Some gangster rap lyrics talk about beating somebody down, beating up spouses, retaliation against other drug dealers and enemies, or just simply being disrespectful and ignorant for no reason. Gangster rapper Lil Wayne spit this lyric: "There's a reason for everythang and my dudes kill for no reason/camo-shorts with a whole beater/all black hoody I'm grim reaper." NWA's Eazy E spit this hook in "Boyz in the Hood": "Cause tha boyz in tha hood are always hard u come talkin' dat trash we gonna pull ya card!" I think these lyrics send a message to adolescents that it's okay to harm someone or take someone's life. This could be the cause for a lot of inner-city youth fighting and killing each other.

Drug use is another influence of gangster rap. Almost all gangster rappers rap about how they relax and chill after a very productive day. Drugs and alcohol are often used to change their mood or just help them to cope with stress. Some lyrics talk about how drugs are cool. Gangster rapper Snoop Dog sings, "Rolling down the street smoking indo sippin' on gin and juice laid back wit my mind on my money and my money on my mind." Nate Dogg sings a hook, "If u smoke like I smoke then u high like everyday and if you azz is a buster 213 will regulate." These types of lyrics can lead adolescents to think using drugs to relax or deal with personal issues is perfectly okay.

Those influences contribute to inner-city youths' criminal activity, violent behaviors, drug use, and many other antisocial problems. Gangster rap is still very popular and controversial. The inner-city youth who embrace this music idolize gangster rappers and want to imitate the thug lifestyle. I think parents have a responsibility to censor what their children and adolescents listen to.

> One evening, in my poetry class, the instructor asked the class to come up with as many words that we could think of that had different meanings. The class came up with quite a few. She then asked us to pick one of those words and write a poem. She gave us five minutes. I chose *hood*. This is what I came up with:

# Hood

I love my hood.
I don't think I'll ever move. Love the atmosphere.
The surroundings stimulate my mood.
I walk when it's hot and throw on my hood when it's chilly.
I hit the hood of the car parked in my favorite parking spot.

# Peace Won't Be Still

They say history repeats itself. Decade to decade that statement clearly speaks for itself.
As injustice prevails, the fire and smoke erupt—riots, violence, destruction, and death. Enough is enough!
No justice! No peace!
Wave the triple Black fist!
Peace won't be still. Killers are acquitted for the killing of unarmed Black men.
It's happening now, just like it did back when lynchings and hangings still existed.
So do bombings, racism, injustice, and prejudice. Peace won't be still.
The scorching smell of fire and smoke.
The sound of crackling, burning buildings fall to the ground.
The raging wave of the raised triple Black fist and the anthem echoes of H. Rap Brown still exist.
"Burn it down! Burn it down! Burn it down!"
God created all men in his image.
God created all men to live for His purpose and glory, so until men live for God's will,
Peace won't be still! Peace won't be still! Peace won't be still!

# Ghosts

The night owls hoot in the darkness as the clock strikes midnight.
Dawning calls for the restless.
They say ghosts never sleep.
They walk, they lurk, they fly, they search to settle unfinished business with guilty souls.
For what's done in the darkness shall surely come to light, so dare to cover your head in the darkness and pray to see daylight.
They say ghosts never sleep.
They walk, they lurk, they fly, they search, haunting guilty souls for closure and eternal peace.

Sometimes my poetry instructor would give our class five minutes to create a poem about something we see sitting right in front of us on our desks. I came up with this poem about my handbag.

# My Cute Little Handbag

You cute handbag you. You're black and colorful too.
Just like me—little, cute, and petite. My mini me covered with my initial.
You really are sharp.
I'm infatuated with your style and much-needed convenience.
You sit quite comfy in front of my desk. I cherish you—so sacred.
Your one of my best.
My cute little purse with the initial of my first name.
It begins with *S*.

# Beautiful Sleep

The pitter-patter of raindrops sing outside morning melodies rhythmically.

The unwelcomed light peeks through a pinch of the drapes slightly. The tired one lays peaceful while at rest.

Nothing can awaken this tired soul. After a long night's labor, sleep at its' best, pillows of comfort cushion the head, and blankets of warmth cover the bed.

An ambience of angels watching and praying, forbidding interruption from beautiful sleep.

# The Sun Will Shine Again

When the birds in the trees don't chirp beautiful melodies anymore; and when the butterflies don't seem to have the welcoming and warming presence you used to adore;
when the wind blows in life's unexpected turmoil, heartache, broken promises,
darkness, and strife; when contention takes its toll, and the soul can cry no more,
the sun will shine again. When the rain goes away, and a tunnel of light above the abyss awaits ashore.

# Birds

Why do birds sing and chirp melodies?
Some melodies are peaceful; some are upbeat and cheerful.
Are they singing because they're happy?
Or is it perhaps they have shelter in their nests?
Might it be they sing because they're free.
Or could it be they're thankful. When trouble and sorrow comes, they can fly high above the skies, far away from you and me.
I'm clueless about what birds do when they fly down south.
Do they mingle on the beaches, or do they settle in tropical forest?
Do they hide in mysterious mountains or caves, or do they fly to the other side of the world? Could it be that birds are visiting relatives when they go down south?
Then after the winter is over in Ohio,
do those same birds return from down south?

# Summer Morning

On my porch, I sit still. I listen to the birds.

As they chirp melodies in their secure nest, the sun slowly creeps up behind the trees.

To greet the summer morning with a sparkling kiss, the squirrels scamper and play across the grass as daffodils and dandelions dance from the light, warm whisky breeze. The natural beauty of nature is priceless and puts my mind at ease.

Every morning should be a cup of cappuccino like this.

# Writing Therapy

When I write, a calming begins. Writing takes me to a new place.
I can write about places of peace and flowing rivers that calm me from within.
I can write about the power of meditation
or the breathtaking vision of diving dolphins and beautiful blue birds as my thoughts serenade my head.
I grasp my pen, concentrate, and write from within.

# Dayton

Dayton, the city beautiful, and home of Paul Laurence Dunbar and
Orville and Wilbur Wright. The city of aviation, technology, and neon lights.
Dayton, a city where innovators, creators, players, hustlers, and the hardworking, too, strive to make this city tried and true.
Where the sounds of Slave, Heatwave, Lakeside, and the Ohio Players came from Dayton, the city beautiful, the bona fide birthplace of funk.
Where Roger Troutman gave birth to the voice box and rocked the charts with Zapp. Shout-out to Faze-O, Aurra, the Werks, and all the bands who put Dayton on the map!

# From the Master's Hands

From the ground, He created a man. From His breath, He blew life into that man. From the mans' rib, He created a woman.

From His gracious mercy, the woman birthed generations through labor. From labor, the man tills the land with the strength God so graciously gave him.

From the earth, man was created, and to the earth man was returned.

> At the beginning of one poetry class, my poetry instructor placed a pair of 3-D glasses, a Costa Rica vase, a whisk, and an Islamic brochure on a table in front of the class. She gave us five minutes to write a poem using all these items. I came up with this:

# Room for Diversity

Looking through the 3-D glasses gives visionary welcoming for cultural diversity.
I vision placing the whisk in the Costa Rica vase and even putting in the Islamic brochure to add to the mixing vase. Cultural diversity is full bloom in this room.

# My Pathway To Success

Anyone who wants to succeed in life must have some kind of pan or map. Success is never easy and can be challenged with many obstacles. My pathway to success will consist of a positive attitude, to get a college education, to continue to work hard, and to be true to myself.

I try to start each day positive. It is never easy working a full-time job and trying to go to school. The first thing I do when I wake up in the morning is take a long stretch and reach for the sky. As I'm walking to the bathroom, I say out loud, "Thank you, Jesus!" That instantly starts my blood flowing and puts my mind in a positive mode. After completing all my morning activities, I pray and ask God to give me all the wisdom I need to make it through the day.

I will not succeed without a college education. I know the job market is scarce. Even though I've been in the mental health field for four years, my job can be eliminated if job cuts start. I am a patient care technician on a mental health unit. If the administrator of our unit decided that only mental health technicians were needed, I'd be the first to be eliminated. I am determined to complete my education and to keep my job. My success depends on it.

I will continue to work hard and be true to myself. I know that I'm a valuable employee. I work hard, and my supervisor and coworkers depend on me. I was awarded a scholarship toward my education from my job. I received two letters of recommendation from two of my supervisors for the scholarship, and both letters bragged about how hard I worked, my positive attitude, and how I am a valuable team member. I will always report to work on time, be an important asset to my job, and always learn something new when I'm working to become a more efficient and helpful coworker.

Success is not always easy. It can be very challenging but worth every obstacle that tries to block it's path. Through failures, hard work, a positive attitude, education, and determination, my pathway to success is obtainable.

# Single Mothers and the Use of Government Assistance

Whether raising one, two, or more children, single parenting is a job in itself. Single mothers who are financially unable to support their children may need temporary assistance from the government. Utilizing government assistance can be a stepping-stone for some single mothers, but for some single mothers it can become a way of life.

Single mothers who choose to seek employment, get an education, or do both can help themselves become self-sufficient. As a single mother of three, I was tired of being on public assistance. After my youngest child turned five in 1998, I went out and found a full-time job. I was able to generate more income in my household. Three years after that, I began to experience more financial stability. As a result, I needed little and then no assistance at all. Now, in 2011, I am getting a college education. In two years I plan to have a degree in mental health. This will help promote job stability and more money.

In contrast, single mothers who choose to remain on the system may never experience better opportunities. For example, a friend I attended high school with now has eight children. Each time one of her kids would get close to school age, she would have another baby. Having these children has made it difficult, and sometimes it's an excuse for her to not seek employment or get an education. She has tried working jobs in the past. Whenever the government started to cut her benefits due to employment, she would quit her job to get her benefits back. She is constantly lacking the financial means to support her household. My friend's dependence on the system has called for other government aid, such as food pantries, United Way, the Salvation Army, and emergency utility programs. She will more than likely be on the system for a very long time.

For many years government assistance was and still is the means of support for many single mothers. Government assistance is temporary relief for single mothers until they financially get on their feet. Consequently, there are single mothers who utilize the system for their benefit, and they become self-sufficient single mothers. The single mothers who choose not to work or get and education continue to abuse the system.

www.ingramcontent.com/pod-product-compliance
Lightning Source LLC
Chambersburg PA
CBHW050047080526
44586CB00014B/1491